If found, return to

MW01537259

Month/Year:

Sunday	Monday	Tuesday	Wednesday	Thursday	Friday	Saturday

Month/Year:

Sunday	Monday	Tuesday	Wednesday	Thursday	Friday	Saturday

Month/Year:

Sunday	Monday	Tuesday	Wednesday	Thursday	Friday	Saturday

Month/Year:

Sunday	Monday	Tuesday	Wednesday	Thursday	Friday	Saturday

Month/Year:

Sunday	Monday	Tuesday	Wednesday	Thursday	Friday	Saturday

Month/Year:

Sunday	Monday	Tuesday	Wednesday	Thursday	Friday	Saturday

Month/Year:

Sunday	Monday	Tuesday	Wednesday	Thursday	Friday	Saturday

Month/Year:

Sunday	Monday	Tuesday	Wednesday	Thursday	Friday	Saturday

Month/Year:

Sunday	Monday	Tuesday	Wednesday	Thursday	Friday	Saturday

Month/Year:

Sunday	Monday	Tuesday	Wednesday	Thursday	Friday	Saturday

Month/Year:

Sunday	Monday	Tuesday	Wednesday	Thursday	Friday	Saturday

Month/Year:

Sunday	Monday	Tuesday	Wednesday	Thursday	Friday	Saturday

Made in the USA
Middletown, DE
04 January 2023

21375992R00073